CLAY PLATES

BROKEN RECORDS OF KISWAHILI PROVERBS

ALEXIS TEYIE

Published by Akashic Books
©2018 Alexis Teyie

ISBN: 978-1-61775-628-3

Printed in China through Four Colour Print Group, Louisville, Kentucky
First printing

Akashic Books
Brooklyn, New York, USA
Ballydehob, Co. Cork, Ireland
Twitter: @AkashicBooks
Facebook: AkashicBooks
E-mail: info@akashicbooks.com
Website: www.akashicbooks.com

African Poetry Book Fund
Prairie Schooner
University of Nebraska
110 Andrews Hall
Lincoln, Nebraska 68588

TABLE OF CONTENTS

Alexis Teyie's collection, *Clay Plates*, opens with a tender anthem of gratitude. The tenderness is achieved through an honest engagement with pain and difficulty. The collection is not sparing in its challenging of patriarchy and the abuses of power; and yet, as a willful act of empathy it begins with gratitude for the moments of human sensibility in the father who functions as a synecdoche of all men:

> My father was the first man.
> A crying father is an impossible thing.
>
> A crumbling face, leathery skin moist,
> eyes small and disappearing, fisted
> hands. I ran my index down his cheek,
>
> I said, *thank you thank you thank you.*
>
> ("Clay Plates")

The poem "Sediments" is even more explicit in its description of the father's hands: "The repercussions of tenderness: / tickle, tickle, tickle!" She is careful to say that her capacity to recover tenderness is an act of poetic magic, if you will: "My heart and I are no longer / on good terms / but I, too, believe in miracles."

The Swahili proverbs—the Methali—that function as epigraphs for these poems introduce us to the sly ambiguity that characterizes much of what happens in Teyie's work, which takes full advantage of the possibilities for capturing the contradictory impulses of human feeling and thought. "Clay Plates," for instance, includes this saying: "The axe forgets; the tree does not."

The generosity of the notes that end the collection offer translations—which in Teyie's hands, have, themselves, the quality of finely wrought poetic aphorisms that serve to further complicate the poems she has written. This is an act of remarkable intellectual deftness, and we are the beneficiaries of these layers of meaning and sentiment.

At the heart of the collection is this engagement with the traditional and the contemporary (what one could fairly call the concerns of African modernity)—a commitment to the retrieval of traditional things in the face of present realities. Often the phrase *this is how it went* recurs—suggesting narrative, but also suggesting a genuine exploration of the nature and value of memory, both for its unreliability and for its necessity. In this sense, Teyie locates herself in a liminal space that is enviable in poets from Africa (who have retained a genuine engagement with the constantly transforming traditional cultures)—the capacity to navigate not just the vexing politics of language, but the rich rewards of modernity rooted in a sense of the past. For her, language is a place of urgent contestation.

Her poem "History is a Loaded Gun" might as easily be called "Language is a Loaded Gun," for in it she writes a meaty exegesis which suggests that language is not simply a matter of national or *mother tongues*. Instead, she expands these to the very act of communication that includes the choice of silence as yet another language—another weapon:

> there is a language
> hollow enough to cower in
>
> large
>
> enough to choke on unsafe
> languages
> sobering distillations

> there are small
> languages pocket-sized
> ready-to-drink languages.

And Baba, the elderly voice, offers the salient wisdom about language:

> *Don't believe all the books*, Baba said.
> Silence is a language you can use,
> but no simpering. Ours is a swimming,

> a rifle of a language.

Teyie is fully aware of the curious compromises demanded from an existence that is postcolonial, an existence characterized by migrations and the navigation of borders, whether they are actual national borders or symbolic borders. "I Hope We Don't Run Out of English" makes clear that on the other side of the border, in the place of exile, English becomes a kind of currency, marked by an anxiety that the failure of language could be dangerous, detrimental. But Teyie is clear that what is at stake are the hopes of those left behind, the hopes of those whose memory is to be preserved by the songs and dances created on the other side, but above all, the hopes of those who will suffer at the knowledge that migration has not been a triumph: "Now that we've crossed the border . . . / Don't write home; don't admit you lost."

It is in this sense that the making of poems becomes its own theme of resistance in the collection. Writing home, in other words, is not merely the business of communicating with family, but the business of writing as an African in exile. Writing home becomes, then, an act of writing about home, inventing or reinventing home, negotiating the meaning of home, and constructing new themes of belonging. In doing this, Teyie is an alert presence. Never accepting things as they seem, she articulates a vigilance that could be called *mistrust*, as suggested in the poem "Non-compliance":

but, don't trust the earth.
don't trust it
with your body, not with
the secrets of your body.

non-compliance is not an option.
the glitter won't save you now,
but here, this is how you terrorize a poem
until it confesses.

With this important foundation as a constant thematic presence throughout the collection, the poet embarks on poems of lyrical intensity and vulnerability—poems that explore the self; the emotional disquiets of relationships between family and friends. In "There it Goes" she allows herself the self-scrutiny to be able to understand that in the face of having been left by a loved one, she is not "radical in her sorrow." Instead, this examination of self becomes cool and clinical: "I say nothing new, nothing different. / My concerns are as they were before: / is the tea too cold to drink?"

But the sense one gets after reading this beautifully organized collection is not one of hopelessness. There are, of course, the splendid anthems of father and mother ("Impact Zones"), which are unsentimental and convincing in their expressions of appreciation. Then there are the intellectually testing works that carry a surrealist's inclination toward self-reflection in the two "Fluid Mechanics" poems: "I, for one, have been researching poems to invoke dramatically upon the moment of my death."

Finally, there is the clear sense of hope in the elegant poem "Water Lilies" that opens with the Methali proverb translated as, "The heart runs deep," which offers a well-crafted expression of defiance against death:

Colour is all that will remain, darling.
Deeply, darkly, but more often, gently,
lightly. Lightly.

And when we are older, we can dream our souls, too,
will leave a residue; paler maybe, but the colour of
water lilies.

The persistence of color is the ultimate expression of hope and possibility. Teyie's work has appeared in various places over the years, and this collection offers an opportunity for us to witness the skill with which she constructs a complex poetics, with echoes and refrains of ideas and a strong sense of assured craft.

In 2015, she famously observed in an essay entitled "Invoking the Women in Early African Writing," that she had formed a list of 770 African women writers, and declared: "If I choose to—and I am seriously considering it—I can subsist on works by African women writers until I expire."

She is a woman who has located herself within the rich tradition of African women writers, and in this chapbook we are witnessing the early stages of what I predict is yet another contribution to that significant number. We welcome this splendid voice.

Kisebusebu na roho ki papo

CLAY PLATES

A man crying alone is ugly.
Uglier than any flower I have
ever seen in any painting.

The list of men I have loved
is long. I write each name
on a clay plate, lovingly.

I place plate over plate, I
resist the counting instinct.
I run my index over the edge.

The clay is cold now, and
a little dry. Now I have built
something. A steeple, a minaret—

the edifice of unseemliness.
My father was the first man.
A crying father is an impossible thing.

A crumbling face, leathery skin moist,
eyes small and disappearing, fisted
hands. I ran my index down his cheek,

I said, *thank you thank you thank you.*

WHERE ALL THE LADDERS START
KISAUNI KUTAMEA MVINDE?

A bad habit of cracking knuckles;
that's the only thing I remember
clearly—
unladylike, vulgar, and so on.

Another memory, a coy one,
this one, lazy and not to be
trusted, but it's mine
so here:

I stole her high platform shoes,
and when she caught me
stumbling about, she
stuffed them with tissues,

and told me, don't let a boy
forget, not even a little,
how much work you are.

THOSE OLD THINGS
KONZO YA MAJI HAIFUMBATIKI

This is how it went, our stolen lullaby.
It went like this:

The tui-tonga bird is not in his usual tree.
It is 6 p.m., and already the *swiiswii* of the sap
is mingling with the *kololo kololo* of your
many dreams, and there is the *huuuhuuu*
of the chickens sleeping, and the *mbulumbulu*
of the knife sharpener's cart going up the hill.
Where is the trilling of our one-legged tui-tonga?

This is how it went, I think.

Memory's soggy with spit;
this is how you put it all together,
that old life of ours.
That's how it went, the story,
the song—where are they now,
those old things?

SEDIMENTS

HAKUNA ROHO KONGWE

Our father was simply a pair of hands.
Folded. Pressed tight. Caressing.
Fisted. Splayed open. Clapping.
All expressive knuckles and
pumping veins, saffron in the sun.

And the repercussions of tenderness:
tickle, tickle, tickle!

My heart and I are no longer
on good terms, but I, too,
believe in miracles.

For instance, a whole face
can find rest in two palms.
For instance, the universe in
the curve of two linked hands is one
in which destiny can be postponed
and fate procrastinated.

BUBBLEGUM DAYS
MOYO WA KUPENDA HAUNA NADHARI

Jojo, how much do I owe those
early threads of love,
those infinite lashes
slinking about me, holding
that first secret suspended
before the shimmering stuff
I saw through and felt through
in our days? And what
did I discover, what was
it, that sly thing I longed for,
and got?

Those bubblegum days, ours,
they were bound to end, no?
Now, another town,
another argument.
A different sun, but
the same old song
on the radio.
When it rains again,
the reflection of your face
sliding down the window is
grainy, knotted—too much
like any other face.

WOMAN, SHAMBLES

DAWA YA JIPU NI KULIPASUA

Now you want to know, I suppose,
how many babies, those
flickering points jockeying to disperse
my smallness, my singleness,
my petty humanness. I suppose
you want to know how many.
How many of those babies
did I kill in my sleep, or maybe
on my way to work, on the bus,
in the shower, silently, me.
The truth is, if you can believe it,
I, too, wonder *when* all those lights
burned in me, beneath my skin.
I wonder *how* those
quivering grains?
The truth.
The truth is, I wonder also
about that stray glitter, those
lost motes,
where.

THERE IT GOES

MAPENZI SI SHURUA, HUJA YAKAJA

The night you leave, the sky breaks out
in stars. They burn like open sores.
The acacia, scarred from private wars,
still has leaves.

I am not radical in my sorrow.
What has come before,
that which has been handed down—
these are my only methods.
I feel what I feel should be felt.
I say nothing new, nothing different.
My concerns are as they were before:
is the tea too cold to drink?

HISTORY IS A LOADED GUN
MOYO NI NYONGO, UKIGEUKA UDONGO

There are small languages
secret ones brazen ones
yielding languages

frigid words

there is a language
hollow enough to cower in

large

enough to choke on unsafe
languages
sobering distillations

there are small
languages pocket-sized
ready-to-drink languages.

Ours was a seizing, a swimming,
a dazzling limp of a language.

Don't believe all the books, Baba said.
Silence is a language you can use,
but no simpering. Ours is a swimming,

a rifle of a language.

SHY FIRES
MWENYE KOVU USIDHANI KAPOWA

To a lover who screams *astaghfirullah*
before exploding all over my carpet, I insist
ecstasy is a central aspect of all faiths. I ask her,
is it me or the joy you find filthy
(an old bruise).

She ends all arguments by invoking
peace upon us. I find this miraculous
(a muddied hope).

That last argument begins with something
on the news, another attack, another
list of people we are too tired
to mourn for. Then something else
about raw mangoes, or the moss
that won't stop spreading.
The final thing is stupid,
as they are wont to be.
All the letters I start afterward
cannot get past the brutal gold
of her nose ring mocking me—
sketches of a stunted miracle.

I HOPE WE DON'T RUN OUT OF ENGLISH

MAJIVU YENYE KUPOA HUUNGUZA NYUMBA

22

Once we get across the border . . .

Leave your fathers and mothers, the lights in the suburbs,
the sullen silences, the hedges, the painted doors.

Once we get across the border . . . we'll dance, dissolve.
Do it for the poems, the songs we sang.

The watchmen know we'll be gone long,
but we have to trust we can fight the sunset.

Now that we've crossed the border . . .
Don't write home; don't admit you lost.

NON-COMPLIANCE
MIOYO HAILINGANI

it all comes down to faulty wiring,
a predilection for silk
and glitter:
an immunity to living.

the last obedient thing I did
was say *aaahh.*

but, don't trust the earth.
don't trust it
with your body, not with
the secrets of your body.

non-compliance is not an option.
the glitter won't save you now,
but here, this is how you terrorize a poem
until it confesses.

IMPACT ZONES (c)
AINGIAYE BAHARINI HUOGELEA

The sharpest memory of your mother
is her in front of a gas cooker.
She is a blown whistle, an unrung bell, a battle ax,
an old heirloom, a new woolen scarf, a white flag.
She is the referee, the priest, the warrior,
the sage, the stylist, the arbitrator.

She held the world together, your mother,
right there in front of a gas cooker.
Holding court. Consulting with the stew, joking.
Holding you up, or down. Holding you close, hoping.
Your mother held the world together with
a handkerchief wet with spit and a safety pin.

Brush fires, bomb blasts, floods, famine.
She's borne it. Whole earthquakes even.
At the impact zone, holding it together.
A woman through all manner of disaster.

AFTERSHOCKS
PATO LA MAHABA NI HABA, HABA

These are the aftershocks of love:
Nanananaaa. Wololo.
We, History and I, are a marimba.
Every time He hits me, the sighs make
a phlegmatic cobalt music.

FLUID MECHANICS
ALIYETOTA HAJUI KUTOTA

1.

You must let yourself sink in comfortably. Without guilt.

2.

I drop everything and stretch out on my bed, chali.
I stare at the ceiling and count my breaths.

3.

You are a being in motion.

4.

I imagine I could drown in myself; my body is 60% water. My brain
is 70% water: we are all swimmers, at least in our heads. Embrace this
fact. But my lungs? 90% 90! This explains the odd bubbling I sometimes feel at the root of me, and I swear when I place my left hand
over the thin skin there I feel a rippling, like a pebble is always being
tossed in. Always upsetting the placid lake. I think of a famous haiku.

5.

When you die, the blood must thrust forward still, due to the force of
inertia. Your veins must bulge outwards; maybe your eyeballs will pop.
Maybe you'll get an erection, aroused by your own self. The first time
you will truly want yourself, you will be dead.

6.

The water in my lungs boils like the hot springs in Lake Bogoria.
I don't know. I am told that sometimes during torture, people are
known to drown in their own vomit. This is not surprising. Instinc-
tively, we must know the ocean always wins. Blame the moon.

7.

Vitreous gel. Aqueous humor.

8.

I, for one, have been researching poems to invoke dramatically upon the moment of my death. Also, I walk around with music playing through my earphones even when I'm not wearing them so my death has a soundtrack, like any proper film. Rejecting the popular, *Do not go gentle into that good night*, I have settled on Stevie Smith: *Not waving but drowning*.

FLUID MECHANICS II

Water is something you cannot hold. Like men. I have tried. Father, brother,
lover, true friends, hungry ghosts and God, one by one all took themselves out of
my hands. Maybe this is the way it should be—
　　—Plainwater, Anne Carson

1.
I wept for 4 hours today. My body is
60% water (or 59% taking into
account lack of sustenance and
menstruation). If I calculate the volume
of one tear drop, and the rate at which I cry (all
things being constant) I might determine how much
of myself I lost, how much is floating outside
my body, surrounding someone else's body.

2.
Crouching in the shower, I remember: I used to lick
the edges of paper before I tore it to pieces.

3.
I tell myself this thing is an oxbow lake,
that I just need to lay flat, follow the thin
estuary to the source. Well, how to swallow
whole oceans ripping out of me? The sand in
all my crevices, is that an accident?

4.
These hands and feet look so old now, so wrinkled;
they must be senile. The salt, it burns my eyes.

5.
All my dreams conform to a certain aesthetic—
dryness. The landscape of my life in
this world is a mosaic of tightly packed
deserts, even the interstices are an optical illusion.
It's possible the world thought me mocking
when I was merely sticking out my swollen tongue,
maybe finally catch a breath.

6.
Else I was a fleeing cuttlefish.

7.
It is equally possible that these impressions
on my neck are from bare feet burrowing,
digging for wells in my throat.
And why not?
All these discrete grains,
their lambent aridness, that clean arrogance,
and its tacit promises heavy with
the tears of things.

8.
Do you know what he said to me? I find
Your lips tender. See, what he meant is, raw.

ASSEMBLY LINE
CHOMBO CHA KUZAMA HAKINA USUKANI

Another funeral I do not have to cry at.

The little boy ahead of me in the queue
to receive communion squirms.
His suit is the colour of sesame seeds.

A woman, his mother I suspect,
spits into a handkerchief,
rubs his forehead as if to erase all petty sins,
any future evils.
She nudges him toward the altar.

Outside, forevers are being orchestrated.
A man crouches next to the barbed wire fence
with his back to the cathedral.
The static on his radio carries.

MEAN DELIGHTS

USUPAOSUPAO NDIO MMEA

Your eyes like freshly blown glass.
Maroon Commandos on the speakers,
a bronze sound.
An ice cube sliding across my clavicle.
Nothing good on TV.
A tender silence, swollen between us,
yeasty and perfumed.

We once knew to take everything we wanted,
without hesitation.
The neighbours' children haven't forgotten.
I can hear them above our domestic din,
taking it all:
Leaves—even dry, even browning, even punctured;
stems and fingers—thin or not, naked and veiled;
flowers—full blossoms, half blossoms, quarter blossoms;
green green buds—at night and in the sunlight.
All of it, they pocketed and plucked and crushed and tossed and not a word,
except the few who spat shards of an old curse—*she loves me, she loves me not,*
she loves me—petals withering in their wake like dead scales.

WITHOUT WARNING
JICHO LA MOYO LINAONA MENGI

Without warning,
the world is yellow again.
What bells blossom, now,
in your mind?

Without warning,
an unpolished joy
staining the horizon:
your many lives ballooning,
resilient globes, in a world
dizzy with yellow.

Unbidden, bliss budding
outside the frame:
when did you become your mother—
sandpapered, urgent, sacred,
redeemable?

WATER LILIES
MOYO NI KILINDI

Colour is all that will remain.

The red of the soil a person
you loved pushes up against.

The yellow of a leaf pressed
between pages in your body's archives.

The black of a pond, a feeling,
mingling with the indigo of a memory

tingling on the edges of your vision:
a child, yours perhaps, laughing an orange-blue laugh.

These are the architectures of your spirit:
the pale of Kisii soapstone, the burn of rediscovered clay.

Colours pulsing up and down
the film of our lives, jolting faces back into place:

Oho! you're Mama Judy's child; and tickling
Fidelity—all our old ideas—out of joint.

Colour is all that will remain, darling.
Deeply, darkly, but more often, gently,
lightly. Lightly.

And when we are older, we can dream our souls, too,
will leave a residue; paler maybe, but the colour of
water lilies.

METHALI

Kisebusebu na roho ki papo
To refuse or relinquish, yet one's heart continues to want. Masking one's eagerness with a false nonchalance.

Shoka husahau, mti hausahau
The axe forgets; the tree does not forget.

Kisauni kutamea mvinde?
How can the mvinde plant possibly grow in Kisauni? Mvinde is native to the Indian Ocean, and Kisauni is a town far from the shore.

Konzo ya maji haifumbatiki
A handful of water cannot be grasped.

Hakuna roho kongwe
No heart is too old.

Moyo wa kupenda hauna nadhari
A loving heart knows no caution.

Dawa ya jipu ni kulipasua
To treat an abscess, cut it open.

Mapenzi si shurua; huja yakaja.
Love is not like measles; it can come back again and again.

Moyo ni nyongo, ukigeuka udongo
*The heart is like gall, or like molding clay.**

---

* This is a little tricky to parse. Other ways to capture this might be: The heart is like bile (bitter or sad), if it changes still more it becomes clay; or, the heart is fickle/malleable.

Mwenye kovu usidhani kapowa
One with a scar, do not think her healed.

Majivu yenye kupoa huunguza nyumba
Cooling ashes burn down the house.

Mioyo hailingani
Hearts are not equal.

Aingiaye baharini huogelea
One who goes into the sea must swim.

Pato la mahaba ni haba, haba
The yield of love is little, is little.

Aliyetota hajui kutota
One who has drowned no longer realizes he is drowning. Or, one who is wet cannot get any wetter.

Chombo cha kuzama hakina usukani
A sinking vessel needs no steering.

Usupaosupao ndio mmea
Is there a plant that flowers without being shaken? Or, to thrive, a plant must withstand the wind's agitation.

Jicho la moyo linaona mengi
The heart's eye sees many things.

Moyo ni kilindi
The heart runs deep.

ACKNOWLEDGMENTS

"Impact Zones (c)" is one section of a three part poem included in a collection of feminist work published by the Heinrich Böll Foundation in 2015.

"Fluid Mechanics I" and "Fluid Mechanics II" were awarded Amherst College's Corbin Prize in 2014 and 2016 respectively.